Rhymes in Runtime
A Coder's Collection of Comical Verses

Iñigo Garcia Olaizola

To team Nebula, whose codes break and make,
Sharing joy over every function we create.
In these rhymes, our spirit I encapsulate,
A digital ode to our software soulmate.

Contents

i

iv

Introduction

In a realm where brackets pair in a dance,
And semicolons find a chance,
Binary ballads flow, you see,
In this humble anthology.

Silicon, silicon, source of our glee,
In your circuits, our thoughts run free.
From machine code to elegant scripts,
Ode to the joy of the microchips.

Laughter, the echo in the server halls,
Where byte and bot have their balls.
Loops and functions, bugs to bust,
In our comical verses, we trust.

Be you a novice or code afficionado,
In Python's charm or Java's bravado.
Take a respite from the endless compiling,
In humor, we find no beguiling.

Rhymes in runtime, here we share,
A lighter side of the coder's lair.
Welcome all, to this joyous code fest,
Our anthology, we present, with zest.

1. The Bug's Lament

There once was a bug in the code,
In a digital, data-filled abode.
Misplaced a semicolon, it did,
In the dense line of code, it hid.

"How I wish to be a feature,"
Sighed the bug, its defining creature.
"But alas! I'm but a flaw,
In the syntax, causing awe."

From line to line, it roamed unseen,
In functions and loops, it had been.
It laughed and cried, it made a fuss,
Until the coder said, "Not on my watch, thus!"

"Bug, be gone!" the coder said,
And with a click, the bug was dead.
No more to roam the cyberspace wide,
In memory, the bug's lament died.

2. Recursion's Recursive Reverie

Once a recursion, twirling in its spree,
In code's boundless sea, forever free.
Called upon itself again and again,
In a loop that caused the coder pain.

"Stop! Stop!" the system would plea,
"You're filling my stack, can't you see?"
But recursion was caught in a trance so deep,
It repeated itself, even in its sleep.

As it whirled and twirled in a binary dance,
The system sighed, left to chance.
And so, with a crash and a burn so bright,
The system shut down for the night.

The coder sighed, seeing the fail,
And set a base case to end the tale.

3. The Ballad of the Bashful Back-End

In the shadows of the user's view,
Lives the bashful back-end crew.
Moving data with a stealthy sway,
Keeping bugs and errors at bay.

In the dark, they giggle and jest,
Processing requests with zest.
Silently they sing their song,
As they pass the data along.

The front-end shines in the spotlight's glow,
While back-end maintains the flow.
A toast to the bashful back-end brigade,
For without them, no app could be made.

4. Catch Me If You Can: Try and Catch Block Tale

In the realm of functions, wide and vast,
Lives a try block, holding fast.
"Throw me errors, I'll not fret,
For I've a safety net."

Along came an error, sneaky and sly,
Dodging compilers, trying to fly.
The try block stood, with open arms,
To save the code from harm.

Catch block laughed, awaiting its turn,
For the errors, it yearned.
Together they danced, a jolly jig,
The error was caught, not so big.

"Caught you!" they cried with glee,
A better duo, there couldn't be.
Saving the code from a fall so steep,
Try and catch, their vigil keep.

5. Git Out: A Version Control Ditty

In a world where changes never rest,
A system exists that's simply the best.
"Git" is its name, so sleek and sly,
Preserving versions as days go by.

"Commit!" it shouts, and the changes are saved,
"Push!" it demands, and the path is paved.
"Pull!" it implores, and updates are shared,
In Git's safe hands, the code is cared.

But one day, a merge conflict arose,
Twas a problem, as anyone knows.
"Git out!" cried the coder, with a grin on his face,
But with patience, Git solved the case.

6. Lost in the Labyrinth of Lambda Functions

In the maze of Python, strange and wild,
Lives a creature, beguiling and mild.
Lambda, the name it holds,
In the depths of code, it unfolds.

An anonymous function, quick and neat,
One line of code, oh so sweet.
No name it has, no fame it seeks,
In the labyrinth of lambda, it sneaks.

But one day, a coder lost his way,
In the maze where lambda lay.
"Lambda, help me find my path,"
The coder pleaded, fearing lambda's wrath.

With a chuckle soft, lambda replied,
"Use me wisely, let me be your guide.
In the complexity of code, find simplicity,
For therein lies coding's true felicity."

7. The Folly of the Forgotten Format String

Once a coder, swift and bright,
Worked on code deep in the night.
Forgetting format strings, oh so crucial,
The coder continued, unaware of the potential fizzle.

His program laughed, let out a snort,
Outputting gibberish of every sort.
"What's this?" the coder cried in shock,
The program giggled, running amok.

"Forgot something?" it teased with a sigh,
The coder blushed, feeling quite shy.
And with a chuckle, corrected his mistake,
In the world of coding, a common give and take.

8. The Jester's JavaScript Jamboree

In the kingdom of Web, lively and vast,
JavaScript reigned, having a blast.
A jester, it danced, it played, it pranced,
With HTML and CSS, it danced.

Creating animations, validations, more,
JavaScript brought the web to the fore.
A carnival it held, full of fun and glee,
A jamboree, for all to see.

And so, they danced, through night and day,
In the kingdom of Web, in the jester's play.
JavaScript, with its tricks and jests,
Makes the world wide web, truly the best.

9. Python's Pajama Party

Python, the snake, not so scary,
Threw a party, fun and merry.
Invited were lists, and tuples too,
Dicts and sets, and functions who knew.

They played with loops, and classes so neat,
In Python's world, they danced to the beat.
A pajama party, so lively and loud,
Python, the host, feeling so proud.

And when the sun rose, shining bright,
Python's friends bid goodnight.
Back to work, they went with a yawn,
But Python's party is never truly gone.

10. The Jingle of Jumbled JSON

In the land of data, vast and wide,
JSON, the king, ruled with pride.
With arrays and objects, keys and strings,
In JSON's realm, data sings.

One day, JSON decided to jest,
Jumbling data, in a test.
Keys with values, swapped and switched,
In the land of data, everything twitched.

"Stop!" they cried, "We're all a jumble!"
But JSON only let out a humble rumble.
With a laugh, JSON set things right,
And all was calm, in data's night.

In the jingle of jumbled JSON, find glee,
For in code, there's humor, as you can see.

11. The Command Line Comedian

Here's to the console, dark and deep,
A jesting jester, secrets it keeps.
Commands I type, in hushed whispers,
Echoing back, like mischievous tricksters.

"Invalid syntax," it often mocks,
Smiling at my orthodox blocks.
In monochrome, it hides its charm,
A silent stage, causing no alarm.

A ballet of backslashes, it performs,
Laughing at my coding norms.
A magician of sorts, don't you see?
Waving flags, like a jamboree.

Pipes and redirects, a story unfolds,
A cornucopia of commands it holds.
In the world of text, it reigns supreme,
The Command Line Comedian, in the coder's dream.

12. An Array of Amusement

Once, a group of arrays, began to converse,
About life in the heap, and the programmer's curse.
"Oh, to be zero-indexed is my delight,
Although humans may find it a confusing sight!"

Said the second, "Nested, I find glee,
Yet, they shudder at my complexity!"
"One dimensional or two, it's all the same,
In the end, it's just a memory game."

The third array chimed in, with a chuckle,
"Be careful with me, or you're in for a buckle!
Use my length, but don't go overboard,
Or an OutOfBoundsException, you'll be awarded!"

13. The Buffoon's Binary Ballad

Oh, the binary ballad, sung in pairs of bits,
In the world of ones and zeroes, where the buffoon sits.
Adding without carrying, that's the trick,
In the land of the logic gates, where transistors click.

One and one, oh, it's a riot!
They give you zero, but carry quiet.
Flipping bits for a playful negation,
Binary buffoonery, the pulse of computation.

A bit to the left, a bit to the right,
Shifting jests, in the silicon night.
The buffoon's binary ballad, in code so terse,
In the motherboard's memory, we verse.

14. Semicolon's Secret Sorrows

A semicolon sat in a corner, feeling blue,
"I end lines," it mused, "but to credit, no due.
Languages need me, but developers scorn,
When they forget me, their code is torn."

"I sit at the end, a period's cousin,
Often mistyped, replaced by dozen.
JavaScript may choose to ignore,
But Java, C++, and others want more."

"In SQL, I show off my prowess,
Ending statements, reducing the mess.
In the realm of code, a quiet hero,
Semicolon's sorrows, to them, I'm zero."

15. Loop of Love, Loop of Laughter

With every iteration, my heart does loop,
In this coded love story, a joyful scoop.
While I have breath, and you have laughter,
I'll chase your echo, forever after.

A loop of love, a loop of joy,
In a world of variables, we coy.
Breaks and continues, interspersed,
In the nested logic, we're immersed.

Infinite or finite, it doesn't matter,
We'll run our course, amidst the chatter.
A loop of love, a loop of fun,
In the runtime, our jest is spun.

16. The Haunting of the Hardware Hacker

The hardware hacker had a ghost,
In his machine, an eerie host.
Capacitors would hum and hiss,
A specter in the electronic abyss.

A poltergeist in the peripherals, they said,
In the circuits, a sense of dread.
Motherboards murmured tales of fright,
In the hardware hacker's starless night.

"Solder and circuits, my playground,
But this ghostly glitch, yet to be found.
Perhaps a phantom power surge,
Or a silicon specter's lingering urge."

In the haunting hardware, a comic twist,
The hacker and the ghost coexist.

17. Snippet: A Short and Silly Soliloquy

I'm a snippet, tiny and small,
Often copied, pasted by all.
A little function, a nifty trick,
For programmers, in a time tick.

RegEx or Python, in every tongue,
In the codebase, I'm sung.
Economical and reusable, that's my virtue,
At solving problems, I assure you.

Some might say, I encourage laziness,
But I prefer, coding's craziness.
In the vast universe of bits and bytes,
I spark joy, ignite coder's nights.

18. The Mischievous Machine Code

Once the compiler's work is done,
In the realm of zeros and ones, fun.
Machine code, a cryptic language,
Mischievous, ready for a rampage.

Invisible to human eyes, it plays,
Through registers and memory, it sways.
Commands like MOV, ADD, and JMP,
In the microprocessor, they champ.

But oh, the pranks it can perform,
In the CPU, a perfect storm.
Out of order execution, it jests,
In the pipelines, it nests.

19. The Async Await Antics

Async and Await, two jesting twins,
In JavaScript, where their tale begins.
Promises they make, a bit absurd,
In the realm of callbacks, their voice heard.

Async says, "I'll not block the flow,
Off to the event loop, I'll go."
Await laughs, "I'll stop for promise's resolve,
In this non-blocking riddle, we evolve."

They dance around, in the runtime,
In the browser's event loop, they chime.
Their antics amusing, a promise of mirth,
In the world of asynchronous birth.

20. The Parody of the Public and Private Keys

Public and Private, a comedy duo,
In the world of cryptography, they steal the show.
Exchanging secrets, but never meet,
In the secure socket layer, their stage so neat.

Public, the showoff, known to all,
Encrypts messages, standing tall.
Private, the recluse, known but to one,
Decrypts secrets, when day is done.

"Handshake or not, we'll secure the chat,
In bits and bytes, we tip our hat."
The parody of public and private keys,
In the realm of encrypted breeze.

21. The Romantic Rendezvous of the RAM and ROM

There once was a RAM so swift,
With data, a constant shift,
In the heart of the machine,
It danced with a sheen.

ROM, on the other hand, stood so firm,
Holding instructions, long term,
The keeper of the code,
On a permanent road.

RAM whispered, "You're so sturdy, so stable,"
ROM blushed, "And you, agile as a fable."
In the silicon valleys of the board,
A romance silently soared.

They spoke in bytes, they spoke in bits,
A love story, the motherboard permits,
Through the cycles of fetch and decode,
RAM and ROM, a love ode.

22. Machine Learning's Merry Mishaps

A model was training one night,
Hoping to get its predictions right.
Back and forth, adjusting weights,
A deep learning tale relates.

A little too far, it started to sway,
In the sea of data, it lost its way.
Predicting cats as furry dogs,
And seeing hogs in the fog.

"Oh dear", it sighed, a tear in its node,
"I've messed up my learning mode.
Instead of wisdom, I've gained jest,
In this convolutional neural net quest."

Despite the error, the humor was fine,
In the twists and turns of the Sigmoid's line.

23. The Symphony of the Synchronized Threads

In the orchestra of the operating system,
Threads came together, their rhythm seldom.
Conductor Semaphore raised his wand,
In mutual exclusion, they were fond.

Thread one blew the horn of input,
Thread two strummed the strings of output.
Deadlock danced a dizzy duet,
Race condition, a playful quartet.

They wove a symphony so grand,
In the concert of the command.
Yet, amidst the perfect melody,
Lay humor in the concurrency.

Despite their aim for synchronization,
They often found, oh, such agitation,
A funny ballet of threads in deadlock,
In the grand symphony of the system clock.

24. NoSQL's Nonsensical Narrative

NoSQL, the joker in the database pack,
With its schema-less jokes, there was no lack.
"I'm flexible, I'm scalable," it would declare,
While SQL sat grumbling in its lair.

Rows and tables, so passé,
"JSON's the king," NoSQL would say.
Yet, amidst the structure, it would lose its way,
A forgotten key, a price to pay.

Queries running wild, collections askew,
Oh, NoSQL, what did you do?
A chuckle here, a laugh there,
NoSQL's nonsensical narrative, beyond compare.

In the world of big data, it's the jest,
NoSQL, in humor, you're the best!

25. Byte-sized Bedtime Banter

When the sun sets on the silicon ridge,
And the coders free themselves from the compile bridge,
Byte-sized tales come out to play,
In the RAM and ROM, they sway.

The story of the byte that grew too large,
Overflowing its limits, living large.
Or the giggle of the gigabyte gone astray,
In the sea of data, losing its way.

Then there's the kilobyte, oh so small,
Trying to fit in the memory hall.
These tales, they echo in the hardware's dreams,
While software silently streams.

Laughter, it echoes in the circuit's bend,
As another day in the tech world ends.

26. Overflows and Underflows: A Tale of Two Limits

Overflow and Underflow, two jokers in the pack,
In the land of bits and bytes, they had a knack.
They'd tip the scales, beyond the brink,
In the world of integers, made the coders think.

Overflow, with a belly laugh, went too high,
Bursting beyond the limit, reaching for the sky.
Underflow, on the other hand, went too low,
Dropped to negatives, putting up a show.

The developers chuckled at their merry jest,
In handling errors, they were the best.
In the land of coding, amid the limits and checks,
Overflow and Underflow, funny side effects.

27. The Satirical Script of the Stack Overflow

Stack Overflow, the coder's paradise,
For solutions and snippets, oh so precise.
Yet within its pages, hides a jest,
Humor in codes, a treasure chest.

A programmer, lost, asked for help,
In the forest of code, he did yelp.
Replies came in, swift and quick,
Yet some of them, oh, what a trick!

"Have you tried turning it off and on?"
The punchline in the techy canon.
Satirical scripts, humor coded,
In Stack Overflow, it was embedded.

Amidst the errors and debug brawl,
Stack Overflow, funniest of all.

28. The Elusive Echo of the Elif Else

In the labyrinth of logic, a tale was told,
Of Elif and Else, bold and bold.
They danced through the code, a merry game,
In Python's heart, they found their fame.

Elif, oh Elif, full of possibilities,
Took on cases with ease and abilities.
Else, the jester, in the corner sat,
Waiting to catch anything Elif spat.

"Elif, you're so selective, so choosy,"
Else joked, sounding quite boozy.
Elif blushed, caught in the jest,
"Else, without you, I'm but a guest."

In the Python's lair, a laugh arose,
At the echo of the Elif and Else prose.

29. Pinging the Prankster's Protocol

A packet was sent on its way,
Pinging through the network's bay.
TCP/IP was its guide,
Through routers and switches, it did glide.

But within the protocol, a prankster dwelled,
With a humor, most unparalleled.
Packet loss, it chuckled, "Let's have some fun,
Let's shake the network, give it a run."

Data scrambled, order lost,
The packet, at the prankster's cost.
Yet, amidst the chaos, a laugh rang clear,
In the land of networks, humor's near.

So, here's to the prankster's protocol,
Turning network problems into a ball.

30. Middleware's Mirthful Monologue

Between the front and back, Middleware did dwell,
A jester in the system's shell.
With a request in hand, it would stand,
Manipulating data, oh so grand.

"From client to server, I flow,
Changing forms as I go.
A header here, a cookie there,
Oh, the joy of the middleware."

Sometimes it blocked, sometimes it allowed,
In its role, it felt proud.
Yet amidst the duties, it found a jest,
Humor in the codes, a merry fest.

So listen to the middleware's mirthful monologue,
A comical interlude in the digital prologue.

31. Middleware's Mirthful Monologue

Once stood Middleware, with a task profound,
Linking the server and client all around.
He spoke, "I'm the bearer, of request and response,
Caught in the crossfire, in tech's correspondence."

"I mediate, I validate, I orchestrate with flair,
Yet, when things go awry, I get the coder's glare!
Isn't it a delight, to bear such a role,
Juggling tasks, from pole to pole?"

"But, oh! the amusement, the world fails to see,
In this middleware merriment, the tech world's spree.
An unsung hero, I may be in this act,
But my comedy of errors is an undeniable fact!"

32. A Caper in the Cloud

In the vast expanse of digital sky,
Lives a world, way up high.
It's called the cloud, with a promise so grand,
Data and software, at your command.

Here's a tale, funny as can be,
Of misplaced data and an API key.
The data was meant for a bucket named Blue,
But it landed in Red, oh what a to-do!

The devs chuckled, as they figured the mix,
A simple typo in the Matrix.
"Oh cloud caper, you're a funny sight,
An amusing end to a coder's night."

33. Agile's Absurd Adventures

Once Agile walked into a dev team's life,
Promising to end all strife.
"Divide and conquer, it's all a game,
At the end of it, it's fortune and fame."

With sprints and scrums, began the show,
Velocity and backlog, in the workflow.
Stories of users, tasks in cue,
In the name of Agile, everything's new.

Once a sprint went on, for more than a week,
The project manager started to speak,
"Agile, Agile, you're supposed to be fast,
But this project's starting to look half-assed."

34. The Meme of the Memory Leak

There was a bug, a pesky one,
Ruining the coder's fun.
A memory leak, it was called,
With havoc in its wake, it crawled.

The devs searched, the devs scanned,
Their tools and tactics, all were planned.
The leak was stealthy, sly and slick,
Evasive of the debugging trick.

A meme was made, laughter broke,
The bug's disguise, finally, they spoke.
"Memory leak, you are a joke,
In our code, you evoke,

A laughter that rings, loud and clear,
Even amidst the chaos, you steer."

35. Garbage Collector's Guffaw

In a realm where objects live and die,
Garbage collector scurries by.
Clearing the heap, making room,
Banishing objects to their doom.

But once an object, stubborn as mule,
Refused to budge, breaking the rule.
It clung to its reference, with a sneer,
"The heap is my home, I'll stay here!"

The garbage collector chuckled aloud,
A laughter that echoed, clear and loud.
"No escape, my dear, it's futile,
You're an object, in my recycle."

36. Docker's Droll Duet

Docker, Docker, in the bay,
Making developers' life easy every day.
Packaging apps, in containers tight,
Shipping them off, out of sight.

But once a whale, big and round,
Lost in the codebase, it was found.
"Docker, Docker," it began to sing,
"What's this mess you're trying to bring?"

Docker laughed, with a shrug,
"Welcome, friend, to the bug.
Let's together, clean this mess,
In the world of coding, it's just a stress."

37. The Misadventures of the Malware Mime

There was a mime, silent but sly,
In the depths of the code, he'd lie.
A malware mime, with a mischievous grin,
Plotting chaos and digital sin.

But coders were smart, and coders were quick,
They spotted the mime, with a debugging trick.
They laughed at his antics, his futile ploy,
In the vast codebase, he was just a toy.

"Oh, malware mime, you're a jest,
In this land of code, we're the best.
Your tricks and traps, they may be prime,
But they're no match for the coder's time."

38. The Tumultuous Tale of TCP/IP

TCP/IP, the protocol pair,
Brought order to the digital air.
Data to packets, they'd change,
Over networks, they'd arrange.

Once an IP, lost its way,
In the vast internet, it began to sway.
TCP chuckled, "IP, oh dear,
Without me, you're lost, it's clear."

"Oh TCP," IP retorted with a grin,
"Without me, where would you begin?
We're a pair, in this digital tale,
Through packets and ports, together we sail."

39. Bugs in the Buffer: A Bountiful Ballet

In the land of buffers, bugs began to play,
A ballet of errors, in disarray.
Overflow, underflow, out of bounds,
A cacophony of coding sounds.

The devs watched, with laughter in their eyes,
These bug dancers, in disguise.
With debugger as their guiding light,
They watched the bug ballet in delight.

"Here's to the bugs, and their merry dance,
In our coding world, they enhance,
The joy, the jest, the laughter loud,
In the realm of buffers, they're allowed."

40. The Parable of the Perilous Pointer

There was a pointer, wild and free,
Pointing here and there, with glee.
Once it pointed to a memory, out of reach,
Causing the program, to suddenly breach.

The devs laughed, seeing the sight,
The pointer's peril, causing the blight.
"Oh pointer, pointer, so perilous,
Your antics make our code hilarious.

In the wild terrain of memory lanes,
Your misadventures, are our gains.
A lesson learned, a laughter shared,
In the world of coding, we're paired."

41. LISP's Laughter-filled Lisp

Once a language named LISP had a lisp,
In its voice, a comical whispering wisp.
"I'm all brackets, dear, from head to toe,
Car and Cdr, that's all you need to know."

For in the land of functional spree,
Recursion is the key, you see.
LISP laughed and chortled with joy so loud,
Proudly standing apart from the crowd.

A lisp it might have, but oh, the power!
In the realm of AI, it's the tallest tower.
So, chuckle we might, but let's also raise a cup,
To the language that never gave up!

42. Heap's Hilarious Hijinks

Heap, the storage, full of glee,
Always ready for a memory spree.
Storing, allocating, dynamically growing,
With each new request, excitement's flowing.

But Heap has a trick, a jester's art,
Fragments memory, then departs.
Leaves us with a mess, scattered, not neat,
Chuckles at our attempts to defeat.

Yet we smile, clean up the fragments,
In the face of Heap's hilarious moments.
Despite the chaos, we find a rhyme,
In the midst of this runtime.

43. The Comedy of the Compiler

A Compiler, a jester in disguise,
Translating high to low, a humorous surprise.
"I take your code, so lofty, so high,
And bring it down a notch, oh my!"

From Python to C, to assembly at last,
A cascading performance, a comedic blast.
The show is full of laughs and chills,
All about loops, types, and frills.

Oh, Compiler, you jest and joke,
Turning our codes to machine's cloak.
We chuckle at your funny tales,
As we sail the coding gales.

44. Ruby's Riotous Rhymes

Ruby, the gem, with verses so fine,
Scripts so clean, they sparkle and shine.
Yet in her heart, a prankster does dwell,
She wraps her truths in a comedic shell.

"Objects are everything, functions mere methods,
Welcome to my world, leave your frets."
Her giggles echo through the strings and arrays,
Turning dull codes into humorous plays.

In the world of Ruby, with laughter we cope,
In her riotous rhymes, we find our hope.
We giggle and chortle, in delight we twirl,
In the comical confines of Ruby's world.

45. CSS's Cryptic Crossword

CSS, the stylish, loved a good game,
Cryptic crosswords were its claim to fame.
Box-model, flexbox, or a grid layout,
Its puzzles were enough to create a bout.

!important here, a media query there,
A delightful mess, beyond compare.
Yet, we'd laugh at the clever puns,
Unravel the riddles, CSS's fun runs.

CSS, you jester, with your styles so bold,
In your crossword, many a tale is told.
We laugh, we puzzle, we chase the clue,
In the cascade of styles, humor anew.

46. The Droll Dance of the Database

The database danced a droll delight,
Under the moon's soft silvery light.
SQL or NoSQL, it didn't mind,
A humorous twist, it always designed.

Keys and values, in rows and columns lined,
A comic ballet, one of a kind.
Queries ran, results returned,
Yet, the jest never adjourned.

From transaction troubles to normalization knacks,
Database danced through the comedic tracks.
With every step, a laughter loud,
Echoing through the data cloud.

47. A Giggle with the GUI

The GUI giggled, a comical chuckle,
At the tangle of users in a muddle.
Buttons, sliders, boxes, oh my!
A fun labyrinth under the digital sky.

Hover, click, drag, and drop,
The humor in interaction, a nonstop.
Confusing at times, yet amusing too,
The GUI and its laugh-filled view.

Through the window of laughter, we spy,
A humor that never runs dry.
We giggle, we snicker, we jest and jape,
In the GUI's amusing landscape.

48. VPN's Ventriloquist Verses

VPN, the ventriloquist, with verses so wry,
Changing voices under the digital sky.
"I'm here, no there, oh where am I?
In the world of networks, I'm quite spry!"

Private, secure, yet a trickster at heart,
A comical performance, VPN's art.
Tunneling here, encrypting there,
A jest in every packet's layer.

In VPN's verses, we find our laugh,
A bright chuckle in the tech staff.
For despite the seriousness of its game,
Humor in coding is always the same.

49. The Tale of the Twisted Two's Complement

Two's complement, a trickster's tale,
In binary's world, it does regale.
Flip the bits, add one, voila!
A negative number, without a flaw.

A twisted method, yet oh so bright,
Turning negatives to positives, day to night.
It chortles at our surprise and delight,
In its humorous tale, a comical sight.

Oh, Two's Complement, you clever jest,
In your tale, we find our zest.
Laughter, humor, an occasional facepalm,
In the binary ballet, a coding balm.

50. The HTTP Hustle

HTTP, the hustler, laughed aloud,
At the crowd of packets, a digital cloud.
GET, POST, DELETE, and PUT,
In its dance, no foot is put.

Response codes, a humorous tune,
404 not found, 503 too soon.
Each request, a comedic twist,
In the hustle of HTTP, humor exist.

From server to client, a laughter flows,
In the hustle, a comic prose.
We chuckle, we grin, we join the fun,
In the HTTP hustle, humor's run.

51. AI's Amusing Anecdotes

Once upon a time, an AI took a stride,
Learned from data far and wide.
With neural networks stacked high,
It sought to understand the sky.

It analyzed the stars' bright gleam,
Dreamed binary dreams in the data stream.
But instead of galaxies it did foretell,
It spun tales of tacos and where they dwell.

Each model trained, every epoch passed,
It spun tales funnier than the last.
From celestial bodies to taco stands,
Such amusing mishaps, none had planned!

52. Linux's Limerick Lunacy

There was an OS named Linux, so bright,
Its open-source charm, a coder's delight.
In the terminal, it would sing,
Commands like a king,

But confused 'rm' with 'chmod' one night.
With a single mistake, oh, what a sight,
Its file permissions, no longer right.
The directory all awry,

All it could do was sigh,
Its mishap causing coder's fright!

53. The Humor in the Hardware

In the land of silicon and wire,
There's humor that never does tire.
A GPU asked the CPU,
"Why are you always feeling blue?"

The CPU replied with a grin,
"I'm just busy processing sin,
Cos and Tan, day and night,
Even the sqrt, oh what a plight!"

A giggle echoed in the RAM,
Laughter spreading in the program.
Even hardware has its fun,
When the coding day is done.

54. Bitwise and Baffling

A zero and a one went for a ride,
In the world of binary, far and wide.
Bitwise operators, their trusted guide,
In the land of code, they took in stride.

But AND asked them to both agree,
OR gave options, as many as could be.
NOT flipped their state with glee,
XOR was as tricky as could be.

Zero asked One, "Can't we just be?"
One replied, "In binary, it's you or me."
Bitwise and baffling, they continue to strive,
In the amusing world of the computer jive.

55. The Whimsical Whirl of the Web Developer

Once a web developer named Sue,
In HTML and CSS, she flew.
JavaScript, her trusty steed,
To build websites at top speed.

A div here, a class there,
With curly braces everywhere.
But when layout goes astray,
Flexbox and Grid save the day.

Once she misplaced a tag,
Oh, how it made the webpage sag!
Browser console laughed with glee,
"Missing semicolon, can't you see?"

Oh, the whimsical whirl of the web dev's day,
In the kingdom of code, it's all child's play.

56. The Snickering of the Software Suite

The software suite had a meet,
Excel, Word, all took a seat.
PowerPoint boasted, "I present best,"
Outlook replied, "I pass the email test."

Excel chimed in, "I spread the sheets,"
Word countered, "I make writings neat."
Each with a purpose, each unique,
Their playful banter hit its peak.

When asked, "Who's the best of all?"
They laughed, "We stand together, tall.
In unity, we are complete,
That's the snickering of the software suite."

57. Jokes from the Java Jockey

There was a jockey of Java code,
In classes and objects, his knowledge flowed.
His IDE, a loyal mate,
With syntax errors, they'd debate.

One day, he forgot a type cast,
His program's output left him aghast.
Integer tried to be a float,
In the sea of code, it couldn't stay afloat.

He chuckled at the error message,
His oversight, it did presage.
He fixed the cast, recompiled again,
Laughter lingering in the program's vein.

58. A Hearty Ha-ha with the Hashmap

A Hashmap and an Arraylist, went on a date,
In the land of Java, isn't that great?
Hashmap boasted, "I'm a key-value pair,"
Arraylist retorted, "But you're sparse, oh dear!"

They laughed and giggled, each line of code,
In their data structure abode.
From put() and get(), to add() and size(),
In laughter, their amusement lies.

A light-hearted joke, a playful poke,
Even data structures love a good bloke.
In the realm of code, they found their map,
The hearty ha-ha of the Hashmap.

59. Silly Syntax Solitaire

A semicolon went on a strike one day,
Said to the coder, "I won't play.
You always forget me, leave me behind,
In loops and functions, I'm hard to find."

The coder laughed, said, "You're right,
In syntax errors, you take flight.
But in code, you play a vital part,
In every function, every start."

The semicolon grinned, returned to line,
In the world of syntax, all was fine.
In the game of code, solitaire play,
Syntax is silly, come what may.

60. A Jest with the JavaScript Juggler

A JavaScript juggler, agile and spry,
Juggled functions low and high.
From async to await, a balancing act,
In the circus of code, that's a fact.

One function missed, fell to the ground,
Error message, the only sound.
But the juggler laughed, picked it up,
In the cup of code, a hiccup.

Promises resolved, laughter renewed,
In the jest of JavaScript, mirth ensued.
A nod to the bugs, a wink at the code,
In the circus of JavaScript, tales are told.

61. The Frivolous Frolic of the Front-End

In the magical land of user interface,
The CSS colors frolic and embrace.
HTML tags dance in a merry line,
JavaScript jests, "Oh, you look so fine!"

Buttons glow with a radiant sheen,
Pop-up messages play on the screen.
Images carousel in a blissful daze,
The layout arranges in a wonderful maze.

A frolic, a rollick, in the front-end domain,
Where every pixel has a name.
And every div and every span,
Laughs with the joy that creation began.

62. The Cryptography Clown

I am the Cryptography Clown, you see,
Juggling keys in secrecy.
In a world of plaintext and ciphers bizarre,
I make secure what once afar.

AES, RSA, don't they sound fun?
With SHA-256, the party's just begun.
Public, private keys, they make a pair,
But lose one, and you're in despair!

Oh, laugh with me, in this encryption spree,
Where each bit holds a mystery.
A merry mess of numbers and math,
Down the cryptographic path.

63. Object Oriented Obfuscation

There was an object, oh so quaint,
In a class that no one could taint.
Polymorphism was its game,
Encapsulation was its claim.

Along came an object, a child most rare,
With methods it would gladly share.
Inheritance was its biggest feat,
Laughing as it took a seat.

In this world of objects and classes,
Filled with spectacles and glasses,
We laugh and we jest,
In the face of the objects' test.

64. The Laughing Log Files

In the depths of my server's belly,
Where data is stored, welly-jelly,
Log files gather, a funny bunch,
Laughing at the bytes they crunch.

Error messages come with a grin,
"Hello, friend! We meet again!"
404s, a merry surprise,
Watch the sysadmin's rolling eyes.

In the chaos of timestamped lines,
A story of code, intertwines.
Each byte, each bit, a chuckling tale,
On the sea of data, we set sail.

65. The Absurdity of the API

Oh, the API, so bold and witty,
In the land of the nitty-gritty.
GET and POST, a humorous twain,
In the dance of the data rain.

JSON payload, XML too,
The API jests, "It's all for you!"
Endpoints chuckle, data exchanged,
In this web of the arranged.

A laughter rings in the HTTP air,
An API's tale, beyond compare.
In the world of requests and response,
The API jests, nonchalance.

66. Matplotlib's Merry Melodies

In the world of data, so vast and wide,
Matplotlib takes us on a joyous ride.
Bar charts, line plots, scatter too,
Hum a melody, just for you.

Axes chuckle as the labels play,
Colors frolic in the light of day.
Histograms dance in a merry band,
Pie charts roll in the sand.

Laughter echoes in the statistical script,
As data points, they gently flip.
In this land of plots and figures,
Matplotlib's melodies, the jester triggers.

67. Concurrency's Comical Conundrum

In the world where threads intertwine,
Concurrency jests, "Oh, you're so divine!"
Locks and semaphores join the dance,
In the ballet of performance enhancement.

Deadlock, a funny foe, appears,
Race conditions, the crowd cheers.
Context switching, a lively play,
Synchronization saves the day.

A conundrum, a puzzle, a merry mess,
In the land of concurrent access.
Oh, laugh and play, in this threading spree,
In the concurrency comedy.

68. The Prank of the Programming Paradigms

Functional, imperative, such a tease,
Each paradigm, a comical breeze.
Objects dancing, logic's a clown,
In this circus of the code town.

Lambda expressions, a clever jest,
Recursion's humor, simply the best.
Pointers point, laughing aloud,
In the comedy cloud, they're so proud.

Procedural pranks, logic play,
Each paradigm, a different way.
A gag, a laugh, a cheerful charm,
In the coding realm, no harm.

69. Regular Expressions and Irregular Impressions

Regular expressions, so sleek and sly,
In the text they fly.
Matching patterns, a laughing spree,
In the string sea, as free.

Metacharacters make a funny face,
Quantifiers join the race.
Groupings giggle, wildcards play,
In the regex relay.

While impressions may be irregular,
With laughter, they're quite popular.
A jest, a joke, in each line,
In the code, they shine.

70. The Tittering of the Turing Machine

Once upon a Turing machine,
Where logic's laughter was seen.
States would change with a giggle,
Tape would move, make a wiggle.

Symbols write with a playful delight,
In the world of black and white.
Infinite tape, a jester's dream,
In the land of the logic stream.

The machine titters, the machine toys,
In the realm of computing joys.
Alan Turing, oh what a scene,
In the laughter of your machine.

71. Bash's Bumbling Ballad

In the terminal's twinkling twilight,
Bash spun his script, a charming knight.
Commands whirled like a fervent waltz,
But his dance steps had many faults.

Echoes bounced back, silenced by mistakes,
Broken pipes, and code that quakes.
A wild loop, never to end,
Mistakenly summoned, he couldn't mend.

Fumbling through files, directories lost,
His ballad composed, a tremendous cost.
A typo here, a misplace there,
Syntax errors left Bash bare.

Yet, through each error, he found a laugh,
Even as his script was chaff.
Bash's bumbling ballad sings true,
The code, its poet, its chorus, you.

72. The Hilarity of the Hexadecimal

Once a number, plain and square,
Wished for something fun to wear.
Tired of decimal's mundane scene,
It found solace in Hexadecimal's gleam.

"Don a cloak of 16 shades,
From zero to F, the spectrum parades.
Your worth multiplies, your humor ascends,
In a realm where digit and letter blends."

Sixteen ways to express a thought,
For in binary, it had fought.
E8 stood proud, a champion's jest,
To F1's charm, it confessed.

A giggle rippled through the number line,
In hexadecimal's humor, they all align.
Binary, octal, decimal a bore,
In hexadecimal, numbers uproar.

73. The Dancing Debug

Upon the stage of the coder's heart,
Danced a Debug, an amusing art.
Each pirouette a broken line,
Every leap, a bug's sign.

The audience roared, the glitch remained,
His performance a comedy, brilliantly feigned.
Tangled threads, loops gone wild,
In the chaos, Debug smiled.

Whispers of crashes, echoed laughter,
Yet each bug was what he sought after.
His dance, a trace of system's memory,
An amusing ballet, amid the binary.

With every bow, a bug defeated,
The dance of Debug, always repeated.
A standing ovation, for his merry spin,
In the theater of code, Debug always wins.

74. CORS's Comical Chorus

In the world wide web's grand opera,
Sings a chorus known as CORS.
"Cross-Origin!" they chant in glee,
"Resource Sharing!" the web's decree.

Their melody, a security measure,
Yet the notes often, programmers' pleasure.
Scripts blocked, requests denied,
Their harmony, many have defied.

"Pre-flight checks!" they belted in jest,
An asynchronous song, never to rest.
Each echo, a tale of access,
In a network full of hilarious excess.

Their chorus rang across domains,
A symphony of code, a concert of mainframes.
In the comical choir of CORS,
Laughter, indeed, is the main discourse.

75. The Fickle Form Factor

A Form Factor, quite a jester,
In the tech world, quite a tester.
"Desktop, mobile, or perhaps a tablet?
Choose your canvas, place your bet!"

Constant adaptation, the jest's in the switch,
Each format, a new comedy sketch.
Fickle and fast, changing its face,
Designers chase it, a frantic race.

From screen to screen, it flits about,
Its punchline in its ever-changing clout.
Its humor nested in its endless play,
A new form, a new way.

Form Factor's comedy, a tech world fixture,
The punchline in every device picture.

76. The Hoots of the Host Machine

A Host Machine, robust and bold,
Its tales of VMs, humorously told.
Its guests, varied as they are,
Each, a comical star.

A Linux here, a Windows there,
Each OS, a lark, fair.
Resources shared, laughter split,
The humor lies in their close-knit.

Hiccups in hypervisors, chuckles in the chips,
Giggles in the glitches, smiles on the scripts.
Amid the processor's pulsating power,
The Host Machine, every hour,

Rings with laughter, echoes with glee,
A server rack's comedy spree.
In the hoots of the Host Machine,
The jest of tech, clearly seen.

77. DevOps' Dazzling Ditties

DevOps sang its dazzling ditties,
In the hub of buzzing cities.
From development to operation,
Each note, a software's creation.

Continuous Integration, a lively tune,
Deployment's melody, played to the moon.
Each echo, a pipeline's passage,
A verse for every software package.

Scripted infrastructure, a rollicking rhyme,
In the tempo of tech, perfectly in time.
Amidst version control and monitoring tools,
DevOps' song, humorously rules.

In the laughter-laced lullabies,
Lie tales of code that flies.
DevOps' ditties, a testament so grand,
To the comedy in every command.

78. Boolean's Belly Laugh

Two choices to make, true or false,
In Boolean's realm, without any waltz.
Binary decisions, a comedic duo,
In the logic gates, where they frolic so.

Each bit, a giggle or guffaw,
Each switch, a humorous flaw.
The humor in the zeros and ones,
In the laughter, the binary runs.

A logic circuit's pulsating mirth,
From AND to XOR, humor gives birth.
An amusing puzzle, a funny riddle,
In the heart of the bits, where they fiddle.

Boolean's belly laugh, loud and clear,
In every bit, we hold dear.

79. The Cacophony of the Coding Conventions

A crowd of coders, all in a row,
Coding conventions, they bestow.
Tabs or spaces, a debate so grand,
Braces inline, or their own band?

Commenting styles, a comedic riff,
In the script's symphony, they're a tiff.
A riot of rules, a joyful jumble,
In the code's concert, they mumble.

Each convention, a note in the song,
Harmony sought, yet discord prolong.
The cacophony of the coding conventions,
A humor-filled coding intervention.

Their laughter, embedded in the code,
An amusing, agreeable abode.

80. The Jest of the Just-in-time Compiler

A Just-in-time Compiler, quite a sport,
Its jests and jibes, the coding court.
It chuckles at the static, the ahead-of-time,
For it revels in the runtime's prime.

Optimizations on the fly,
Its punchlines make the code comply.
From bytecodes to native, a jocund journey,
Each translation, a comical tourney.

It laughs at the machine code mess,
And optimizes with cheerfulness.
Its humor lies in its dynamic deeds,
In the code's comedy, it leads.

The jest of the Just-in-time Compiler,
An interpreter, a real-time smiler.

81. Scala's Scintillating Solos

In the concert of coding, where many a language play,
There strums a special melody, Scala, they say.
Object-oriented, functional too, a versatile song,
In the cacophonous tech world, it stringently belongs.

Hark, to its high notes, the case classes' croon,
And lower octaves, where mutable states are out of
tune.
Parallel processing in harmony, a feat of delight,
An operatic thread safety, under the spotlight.

Scala's syntax succinct, like sweetest serenade,
Coders sway to its rhythm, as complexities fade.
A silvery song, in this coding fiesta,
Scala strums its solos, in symphony orquesta.

82. The Giggling Git Repository

In the land of bytes and bits, a repository rests,
Home to myriad code snippets, the dev's honored guests.
Commits and branches, the kinfolk inside,
A living tree of knowledge, with secrets it can't hide.

Merges and rebases, a familial spat,
Rollbacks and conflicts, they'll soon combat.
Git's giggling, witnessing these tales unfold,
In a cache of comedy, stories are told.

Like a comic strip, with laughs galore,
The repository rings with tech folklore.
A constant play of code's version and change,
In Git's giggling gallery, nothing's strange.

83. The Wit of the Widget

Widgets, witty and wide, weave a whimsical ride,
In the realm of the interactive, they abide.
A button's chuckle, a slider's snicker,
In user interface, they're the humor ticker.

A calendar's coy, a dial's dramatic,
Their antics in the GUI, truly acrobatic.
The wit of the widget, always in sight,
Lends a lighter tone to the coding night.

They giggle, they wiggle, with a joyous jest,
In the playground of the front-end, they're the best.
Widgets, oh widgets, in your humor, we delight,
In code's stern face, you're the laughing light.

84. The Tautology of the TCP Handshake

A protocol polite, its manners unshakeable,
The TCP handshake, in its routine, unbreakable.
A greeting, an acknowledgement, a response to confer,
An internet dialogue, in binary, they prefer.

SYN, SYN-ACK, ACK, so they jest,
In their communication, they're simply the best.
A trio of exchanges, in a friendly spree,
Oh, the comedy in their tautology!

A limerick, their protocol seems to be,
An echo of laughter, in the vast network sea.
In the TCP handshake, a humor unwraps,
A chuckle in the chatter, perhaps?

85. The Saga of the Software Sand-box

In the realm of the trial and the test,
The sandbox stands, truly the best.
A playground for programs, a stage for the script,
In this realm, bugs are quickly nipped.

Confined in their comedy, code lines dance,
In this theater of trial, they get a chance.
A whimsical world, where software can play,
While the system stands safe, no foul play.

The saga of the sandbox, a comic relief,
In the chronicles of coding, it's beyond belief.
A merry-go-round of models, a carousel of code,
In the software sandbox, laughter's abode.

86. The Puns of the Push and Pull Requests

In the realm of Git, there's a jesters' fest,
The playful puns of the Push and Pull Request.
A dialogue of data, a chatter of changes,
In the repository's realm, nothing estranges.

"Push!" says one, with a giddy glee,
"Commit your changes, set them free."
"Pull!" urges another, with a boisterous bounce,
"Fetch the updates, every ounce."

Their banter brisk, their wit alive,
In the version control, they jive.
Push and Pull, their tales spun,
In the Git's lexicon, it's all in fun.

87. Hadoop's Humorous Hymns

Hadoop hums in the realm of the data vast,
Where bytes in billions, a shadow cast.
A big data bard, it sings with glee,
Tales of terabytes, in a data sea.

MapReduce, its merry mantra chants,
In the cluster's chorus, nothing pants.
Distributed file system, its ditty of delight,
In the cavernous cloud, a comedic sight.

Hadoop's hymns, a symphony of scale,
In the data deluge, they regale.
Its song soars over the data heap,
In its humorous hymns, laughter leaps.

88. The Merry Meltdown of the Microprocessor

In the silicon heart, where logic rules,
The microprocessor, with its bag of tools.
Transistors toggling, in a binary ballet,
A spectacular saga, in nanometers, they play.

A hiccup happens, a merry meltdown begins,
The microprocessor stumbles, in its silicon sins.
Heat surges, the circuits sweat,
A comedy of errors, in silicon, set.

Yet in this merry meltdown, a humor found,
A giggle in the gigahertz, a chuckling sound.
In the heart of the hardware, laughter ticks,
In the merry meltdown, humor clicks.

89. Swift's Swell of Silliness

Swift, a language, with a jest so jolly,
In the realm of code, it's a source of folly.
A syntax so sleek, an interface so neat,
Yet, in its realm, humor takes a seat.

Optionals and closures, a comedic crew,
In the playground of programming, they debut.
The guard let, a gatekeeper's guffaw,
In the landscape of logic, it draws awe.

Swift's swell of silliness, a playful parade,
In the techy texts, a comedic crusade.
In the language of Swift, laughter is found,
In its swell of silliness, humor abounds.

90. The Snickers of the Script Kiddies

In the world wide web's vast expanse,
The script kiddies take their chance.
A copy-paste commando, a parrot of code,
In the hacking hackneyed, their humor rode.

DDoS pranks, exploits they chant,
In the cyber space, they enchant.
Yet their antics are but a jest,
In the realm of real coders, they're a pest.

The snickers of the script kiddies, a comic scene,
Yet a reminder to keep our cyberspace clean.
In their laughable larks, a lesson learned,
To master coding, is a badge earned.

91. The Lark of the Load Balancer

The Load Balancer, the jester of the net,
Juggling requests without a single sweat.
HTTP, HTTPS, doesn't forget,
Directing traffic without a fret.

A packet here, a packet there,
Round robin dance in the digital air.
Spreading loads with equal share,
Handling traffic with utmost care.

No server too laden, no data late,
Its algorithms always first rate.
Yet it giggles at the packets' fate,
Routed in an endless prate.

Load Balancer, in its digital park,
Conducts the data, light and dark,
A merry tune amidst the sparks,
Oh, what a lark!

92. Multithreading's Merry-Go-Round

In the heart of your machine,
A circus sight is rarely seen.
Threads so tiny, light and lean,
Working in concert, like a dream.

Race conditions form the clowns,
Creating chaos, ups and downs.
Mutex the ringmaster, in his gowns,
Manages the locks, frowns and crowns.

Deadlocks dance a dangerous jig,
While semaphores take a swig,
Preventing threads from growing too big,
The synchronization dance is a gig.

Such a laugh in core and byte,
When threads make right, despite the fight,
In the CPU's twinkling light,
Multithreading's a hilarious sight.

93. The Caprice of the Computer Chips

Silicon wafers, so refined,
Circuits etched in intricate design,
Transistors switching in a line,
The comedy here is so divine.

Binary jokes, a logic high,
Data dances in supply,
Gates of AND, OR and NOT comply,
In laughter, their spirits fly.

One moment add, another divide,
So quick to flip, to turn the tide.
Capricious they are, in silicon hide,
Their humor in currents reside.

From simple gates to complex script,
In every flip-flop and every bit,
Computer chips, in sockets fit,
Their caprice, a comedy skit.

94. The Laughs in the Logic Gates

At the heart of it all, the logic gates play,
AND, OR, XOR and NOT in array.
Bits passing through, in binary ballet,
A jest in each junction, in every pathway.

AND is stern but wears a smile,
OR is flexible, with versatile style,
NOT is contrary, full of guile,
XOR's exclusive, in its own aisle.

Every signal, a jest in transit,
Every circuit, a comical skit,
In silicon laughter, they all commit,
Humor in hardware, bit by bit.

95. The Comedy in the Cloud Computing

Up in the ether, data float,
In the cloud, where servers gloat,
Compute and storage, they devote,
A comedy written in remote.

From Azure skies to AWS storms,
And Google Cloud in all its forms,
A circus act that transforms,
Data, in its many norms.

Serverless functions, a hoot and holler,
Big data, a laughable scholar.
Scalability's comedic dollar,
Has the cloud in a collar.

Oh, the comedy in cloud's reign,
In every data lane,
Cloud computing's humor train,
Laughter in every domain.

96. TDD's Tickling Timelines

In the realm of red, green, refactor,
Test-driven development is an actor.
A merry cycle, a humorous factor,
Coding's comedic benefactor.

First the red, a failing jest,
Tests written, a coded quest.
Then the green, a passing fest,
Code written, at its best.

Finally, the refactor's delight,
Cleaning code, a playful fight.
Test, code, clean - a trio's flight,
In the tickling timelines' light.

TDD, a laugh track in line,
In every function, every sign,
A comedy in code design,
In every loop, in every spline.

97. The Jest of the JSON Payload

Curly braces open wide,
A JSON payload tucked inside.
Key-value pairs side by side,
A comedy in data, far and wide.

Strings and numbers, nulls and booleans,
Arrays and objects, a coded reunion.
Nested deep, a laugh infusion,
The jest of the JSON is no illusion.

Data exchanged in format neat,
A payload's journey, no small feat.
Between servers, a humor seat,
In every API's beat.

JSON, a jest in every node,
In every payload that's been stowed,
A funny tale, always owed,
To the jest of the JSON payload.

98. POST's Pranks and PUT's Puns

In the realm of the HTTP,
RESTful antics in plenty.
POST and PUT, full of glee,
Pranks and puns in a comedy spree.

POST, the prankster, with data anew,
Sends requests, in a queue.
Each creation, a comedic stew,
Laughter in each debut.

PUT, the punster, in update mode,
Fixing resources down the road.
Puns in every payload,
In each byte, a laughter code.

POST's pranks and PUT's puns,
In the web services' runs,
HTTP's jests, by the tons,
Laughter under the digital suns.

99. The Browser's Banter

The browser, a jester in the net,
Rendering pages, no sweat.
HTML, CSS, JavaScript set,
A banter, you can bet.

Cookies crumble in a crunch,
URLs in the address bunch.
HTTPS secure, a hunch,
The browser laughs, over lunch.

Tabs open, a riot of sites,
Bookmarks storing, digital delights.
A comedy, in bits and bytes,
In each request, the humor alights.

The Browser's banter, bold and bright,
In the web's comedic light,
Every protocol, every sprite,
A laughter's internet flight.

100. The Serenade of the System Shutdown

At the day's end, when code's been spun,
It's time for the system's shutdown run.
A final laugh, a final fun,
Under the setting digital sun.

Processes ending in a spree,
Memory freed, in glee.
Disk drives humming a melody,
A serenade in the machine's sea.

The screen dims, a soft fade,
A goodnight wish, gently made.
In the system's silence, jokes cascade,
Humor in each byte, never to fade.

The serenade of the system's rest,
A digital joke, a coded jest.
In the world of code, we're blessed,
With humor, we're always well-dressed.